D0726420

THE NEW FOREST

Above The Crown and Stirrup, traditional symbol of the New Forest and badge of the New Forest Show Society.

Following page Commoners' stock grazing Longwater Lawn.

THE NEW FOREST

A PORTRAIT IN COLOUR

PHOTOGRAPHS BY TERRY HEATHCOTE

TEXT BY JACK HARGREAVES

DOVECOTE PRESS

The Lymington River in autumn.

First published in 1992 by The Dovecote Press Ltd
Stanbridge, Wimborne, Dorset BH21 4JD

ISBN 0 946159 91 2

Designed by Humphrey Stone

Photoset in Sabon by The Typesetting Bureau Ltd, Wimborne, Dorset
Origination by Chroma Graphics (Overseas) Pte Ld, Singapore
Printed and bound by Kim Hup Lee Printing Co Pte Ltd, Singapore

British Library Cataloguing-in-Publication Data
A catalogue record of this book is
available from the British Library

CONTENTS

FORDINGBRIDGE
R. TEST
SOUTHAMPTON
LYNDHURST
BEAULIEU RIVER
RINGWOOD
RIVER AVON
RIVER LYMINGTON
BEAULIEU
BROCKENHURST
AVON WATER
LYMINGTON
CHRISTCHURCH
THE SOLENT
THE NEW FOREST
0 1 2 3 4 5 10
MILES

THE NEW FOREST

In the beginning Forests had nothing particular to do with trees. They were wildernesses, the land furthest from human settlement, and as the population grew they were kept in the wild state as hunting-grounds for the King.

In 1066 William of Normandy eagerly took over the Saxon Forests. Hunting was his sport, and also a continual necessity for the feeding of his huge retinue as it travelled the land to govern and impose obedience. Indeed – unsatisfied by the Forests of Sherwood and Dean, Ashdown, Gillingham, Epping, Arden and many others – he seized upon the coastal land of Ytene, which had been a territory of the Jutes, and declared it his New Forest. This was the act of a Conqueror. It must have caused great hardship to return to the wild a land where people were already settled.

Hardship was usually close at hand for the cottagers who continued to live in the Royal Forests. Although they were protected by the Common Law of the land, which even under feudalism was constantly being developed to see justice done at all levels, the separate Forest Law of the Norman kings took precedence. Its laws were harsh and its punishments savage. A man could be hanged for killing a deer, and no dog large enough to harry a deer could be kept in the Forest unless it was crippled by striking off the toes. Forest Law was not designed to give people a full and prosperous life, but to protect the King's deer and wild boar, the hare and all the creatures of his hunting ground.

For eight hundred years the Royal system ran. No one had the right to question it. Naturally in all that time there were changes. Gradually the more fertile parts of the Forest passed into private hands. Successively the varieties of deer increased. Now probably all the kinds of wild deer in Britain live close at hand in this one place.

With the beginnings of industrialism charcoal burners set up camp in the Forest and shiploads of their product left Lymington for delivery to the early iron foundries. As Britain grew into a world power groves of oak trees were planted to be cropped to provide the timber for the Wooden Walls of the Royal Navy. Indeed Nelson's own first flagship was built on the very shore of the Forest at Buckler's Hard. Stallions of various breeds, from Arab to Hebridean ponies, were turned out with the Commoners' mares by well-meaning people so that the New Forest Ponies became more various in type and size and colour than any other native breed.

Gradual changes such as these, however, made no difference to the political state of the Forest. That held fast, in principle, through the reigns of thirty-three monarchs to whom the crown passed since William the Conqueror. Then, in the latter half of her reign, Queen Victoria announced that she was no longer concerned with the King's deer. An Act was passed for their removal from which they have only recently recovered. In a series of subsequent legislation the Forest passed to the State and its management to the

Forestry Commission. The Court of Verderers were confirmed in the task of overseeing the continuing rights of the Commoners.

Although the Forest had now become a public place it seemed in no hurry to change. When I first pitched a tent there in 1928 the place still seemed remote and undisturbed, though plantations of conifers were becoming evident as the Forestry Commission sought to carry out its remit to operate at a profit. But even after the Second World War there was no defined limit to the Forest. In the winter when grazing was short the ponies wandered out down the road verges and ravaged the gardens in Totton village alongside Southampton. People could still drive their cars across the land. A family could pitch camp among the gorse and bracken and never know that their enjoyment had kept the Dartford Warbler and the Red-backed Shrike from their nests. In the nineteen sixties the boundaries were first fenced and cattle grids built to keep the animals inside. Car parks began to be made and sites organised for camping and caravans. Yet, living then in the middle of the Forest, I could still drive my pony eighteen miles to Ringwood Market and put foot only twice on made-up road between home and the market town.

In recent years that has changed, and now more than 18 million people live within an hour and a half's journey of the New Forest – a Forest which now belongs to each of them as much as to any other. Many of these people annually cross its boundaries for a hundred different reasons. To find a quiet life in the country or to organise a sponsored walk; to ride their own ponies or to feed the wild ones; to play cricket on the 'lawns' or to fish the Forest ponds; to follow hounds after buck or fox or hare, or to protest about hunting; to walk the dog or to round up the cattle and bring them to the pounds for branding; to seek out an hour of rural peace and quiet, or to shatter it with the howl of model aeroplanes. Children come with their teachers to learn, and others with their parents just to run free of traffic.

On top of that tussock-sedge an adder lies coiled in the summer sun. Alongside the peat-hag a crawling naturalist searches for the Fairy Shrimp. A retired senior soldier pursues along a fallen log a rare kind of beetle. The lady with the binoculars is scanning the fuzz and bracken for the sight of a Dartford Warbler; and the man who is so long motionless with his back against a tree is hoping that one day through the long grass will pass the hump-back of a Barking Deer. In the evening the baby badgers will creep cautiously down to where the family picnicked, and be rewarded with a treasure of spilt 'Smarties'. On any day a multitude of things are happening in the New Forest. The pictures in this book were chosen from thousands of photographs, many of them specially taken. As many more could be taken, but these – colour-printed to perfection – bring to life wonderfully the remarkable legacy that has been preserved through forty reigns. The largest and most perfect stretch of wilderness remaining in Southern England.

The New Forest now confronts problems that are critical. The simplicity of government that preserved it so long unaltered has been exchanged for all the complications of democracy. The Foresters were a private people sharing a common existence. Now all of the people with all their life-styles and diverse notions of entitlement have become the shareholders. It is an opinion of my own that if we can govern the New Forest equitably and still preserve its true identity then democracy can govern anything. Can we enjoy the New Forest and keep it? I hope that those who turn these pages are encouraged to find the will and the heart to do so.

JACK HARGREAVES

THE GREENWOOD

THE GREENWOOD

It has been said that the world would still be all covered with trees if man had not come down out of them.

Through the long ages of prehistory a vegetable covering had grown over the Earth, varying and developing with the climate, the degrees of humidity and the emergence of different species.

After the last Ice Age there spread around the temperate areas of the Northern Hemisphere the woodland species we know now. It is now called Temperate Forest. In the early language of our people it was known as the Greenwood.

It all happened slowly. It is now possible for scientists to retrieve the tree pollen which has lain entrapped at various levels of the soil and to discover the age of it. They know that the alder trees and the birch came early in cold, wet times; that the oak came later, and later still the beech.

Previous page The entrance to North Oakley Inclosure, neatly showing the two types of woodland that give the New Forest its character. North Oakley Inclosure was enclosed and planted with oaks in the mid-nineteenth century and is one of a hundred deliberately planted inclosures, whilst the beech in the foreground stands inside the 'natural' pasture woodland that makes the New Forest so unique.

A Grey Squirrel enjoying a breakfast of hawthorn berries. The Grey Squirrel came late to the Forest, not until the 1930s. Its rise may have coincided with a periodic outbreak of viral infection in the Red Squirrel, which left it unable to recover once the bigger and stronger Greys took over. In its heyday the Red Squirrel was often eaten, as in America, and even sent up to Smithfield Market. The lead tops of the throwing sticks used to to hunt them are still sometimes found under the trees.

Old oak woodland, the 'driftway' between Hawkhill and Frame Heath Inclosures. The 'driftways' date back to the plantings in the 18th century, when gaps were deliberately left so that stock could be moved or rounded up. Along with the beech, the oak is the classic Greenwood tree. From the early 18th century onwards New Forest oaks provided ever-increasing quantities of timber for the Royal Navy. In 1805, the year of Trafalgar, it was estimated that one and a half million oaks were at sea in ships of the British Navy.

Britain still had much forest when the Conqueror arrived. Our own chosen area, which nine hundred years ago was also his choice, was already settled as a place of small scattered hamlets. Lyndhurst, Brockenhurst, Minstead, Burley and Boldre were already manors. But even then the New Forest contained great stretches of Greenwood, which the Normans called the Vert, and was the habitat of the wild deer, the Venison.

Hunting was the favourite sport of the early Kings and, indeed, the Norman Kings had strict rules and customs for practising it – as huntsmen tend to do. For instance, deer could never be shot with the 'barbed' arrows of war lest they only be wounded and escape to die in lonely places. 'Picket' arrows – plain pointed ones – were to be used by the royal hunting parties.

But these were just diversions, no doubt carried out with some grandeur. In fact, the Norman Kings needed deer in much greater quantity than a day's sport could provide. If you walk in the Vert today you can still see traces of how the New Forest was turned into a great deer ranch.

Mature beechwood in May. The beeches came late to the Forest, following the limes, which paid for their palatability and were grazed away. They found ample room because they grow on poorer soils than the oaks. Their light-excluding canopy keeps the ground bare underneath.

An old cast iron Inclosure Marker at Rhinefield Sandys Inclosure. It was put up by Gerald Lascelles, Deputy Surveyor between 1880- 1915, and the 'ER' at the top stands for Edward VII. These old Inclosure markers are quite rare. The 'Thrown Out' means that the fences were taken down in 1840 because the trees inside the inclosure were big enough to withstand browsing.

The remains of the old inclosure bank at Backley Inclosure. The bank was originally 6 feet wide with a ditch on the outside. It was topped with split oak palings and a high thorn fence was planted on the inside. Though a maze of such relics survive, very few still boast the stumps of the thorn. The original bank may have had 'deer leaps' so that the cattle couldn't pass, or might have been constructed to guard trees for the king's foresters to fell.

Winter sunrise in the Ancient and Ornamental Woodland at Marsh Ash, an area of the New Forest sadly much devastated by the storms of the last few years. The phrase 'Ancient and Ornamental Woodland' was the title given to the old Greenwood by the New Forest Act of 1877, known locally as the Commoners Charter, and the first legislation to recognize the importance of preserving the natural beauty of the New Forest.

The badger is common in the Forest, and probably always has been. Brockenhurst, or 'badger-wood', dates back to the Saxons. The badger's staple diet of earthworms is not particularly plentiful, due to the acid soils, but they compensate by eating fungi, acorns and berries. This is a typical New Forest badger sett, on sloping ground just inside the edge of a wood.

A vixen with her three-month-old cubs outside their earth. Foxes are not numerous in the Forest, though there are sufficient for fox-hunting to have continued. In the time of William the Conqueror there were bear, wolves and eagles to threaten the young deer, but a fox can still take a sickly baby deer if food is short - though they find it easier to breed near the villages so as to be able to raid dustbins!

The rarest of the Woodpeckers, the Lesser Spotted, clings alongside its hole after returning with food for its young. The shrub-nesting birds don't really flourish in the hard-grazed forest, and the old pasture woodland is dominated by hole and crevice nesters - Nuthatches, Redstarts, Treecreepers.

A Tawny Owl, by far the most numerous of the owls in the Forest. They have to work hard for their living, as they prefer hunting in scrub. I like to think of the Tawny sweeping to and fro in the dark after the mice moving across the smooth floor of the woods.

Left Autumn colour amongst the beeches at Church Place, with natural regeneration visible in the background. The oldest beech trees in the Forest date back to the early 17th century.

Opposite page Beech in late summer, mature trees that grew up naturally amongst older ones now cleared away.

Left A Silver-washed Fritillary posing with the bloom on which it loves to feed - the bramble. The strong, fast flight of the Silver-washed Fritillary makes it the most noticeable of the woodland butterflies in July. It is normally found in the fenced inclosures, where deer and livestock are unable to get in to feed on the ground vegetation.

Below There are fewer wild flowers under the trees in the open Forest than in other areas of English woodland, for the ground is too hard-grazed for flowers such as bluebells to flourish. However, thanks to the large quantities of dead and rotting timber, over a thousand varieties of fungus grow in the New Forest, including the highly poisonous Fly Agaric, here seen in early autumn growing beneath Silver Birch.

Below The beech woods at Mark Ash.

A Forest pony browsing on holly in Matley Wood. Holly is a common source of winter food, and can often be seen browsed like this one - just up to the height that ponies and deer can reach. Hollies either grow beneath the larger trees, as here, or form clumps out on the heathland, where they are known as 'hats' or 'holms' - a name that has always been common on maps of the Forest.

Early morning dew lit up by a sudden shaft of thin wintry sunlight in Brinken Wood.

THE VENISON

The importance of the wild deer to the mediaeval gentry lay in the fact that they are 'browsers' – that is to say they nibbled at the shrubs and the underwood plants, particularly in winter, eating ash shoots, holly and hawthorn, tree-bark, ivy and fungus. The cattle, which were 'grazers', could not be kept in any quantity through the winter, except for the few beasts that had survived smoking or salting (and no doubt the taste for spices and strong flavourings arose from the fact that such meat had not survived too well).

The deer however, even though their condition might be poor in the hardest season, were there to provide fresh meat on the hoof all the year round. So they became the perquisite of the powerful.

The King, having taken care to settle his fractious barons on estates far apart in order to prevent too much power gathering in one place, was constantly travelling the country with a great retinue and a strong force of soldiers in order to keep the peace and carry out the act of ruling. Days ahead of him would ride a herald carrying to the Forest a Deer Warrant calling for the collection of the venison that would be needed to feed his host.

I think that three kinds of deer would have been available to His Majesty. The big Red Deer – the famous Monarch of the Glen, then living in the lowland habitats though now driven to the mountains and moorland – survives in the New Forest in a population of about 150. The Fallow Deer, favourite of the Normans and as it numbers about fourteen hundred the most numerous today, with spotted summer coat and palmate antlers. The little Roe Deer, hardly larger than a sheep, the most beautiful deer, producing the tastiest venison, was probably rare in William's time and may even have died out to be later re-introduced. Latterly its numbers have sharply increased to about three hundred..

More recently the Forest has gained the handsome Sika Deer, and just once I have seen the tiny Barking (or Muntjac) Deer. This is not unexpected since it creeps head-down through the tallest grass. But quite often at night I have heard its sharp barking call repeated every few seconds for ten minutes on end.

I know one man who is sure that we also have the Chinese Water Deer. It is possible, for it is easy to mistake for the Barking Deer and its cry is similar though a little wilder. Recent sightings have confirmed that it is undoubtedly getting closer, and it is spreading fast over the country, so the New Forest might well contain all six species of deer.

Previous page A Red Deer Stag, the largest of Britain's land mammals and, with the Roe, one of our two native species. The stag's antlers increase in size and complexity every year, reaching full development in the sixth year. A stag with twelve points is known as a 'royal' and might weigh as much as 15 stone. The Red Deer in the Forest are good at keeping hidden, but, in the autumn, the deep roaring bellow of the stags' mating call can be heard at great distances. They are mainly to be found in the southern woods and the central heart of the Forest.

A pair of Red Deer hinds, ears raised in alarm.

Left The 'Heir Apparent' - a Red Deer stag in the morning mist. When I first knew the Forest you could almost count the Red Deer on your fingers, a situation made worse when someone defiantly shot the leading stag for marauding on his crops. In 1962 twelve were released north of Burley and, together with those already surviving in small groups, the population has now built up to about 150.

Below Red Deer in autumn. They are just starting to moult and their brighter summer colour is giving way to the more subdued winter coat. The rut takes places in October, with the stags then fighting for supremacy over a troop of hinds - which the stag in this photograph is now keeping a close watch over.

Fallow Deer grazing at sunset on Backley Holmes, an area of lawn reseeded in the 1960s to improve the grazing for ponies. The earliest known reference to the numbers of fallow in the New Forest is for 1670, when there were more than 7,500. Their numbers declined dramatically following the Deer Removal Act of 1851, when a deliberate attempt was made to increase the enclosed forestry at the expense of the deer, but their population has gradually increased, and is now maintained at about 1,400.

Fallow bucks feeding in a woodland clearing. They mainly eat grasses, herbs, shrubs and fruit, but heather, acorns and beech mast are an important part of their winter diet. They feed during the evening and night, especially if moonlit, and also at daybreak as they move to their daytime resting place. In the New Forest it is more common to see the does than the bucks. They graze in the open, and can sometimes be spotted in the heathland valleys or on the more secluded lawns.

Fallow Deer bucks in early autumn, shortly before joining the does and taking their places on the 'rutting-stands'. Each year their new antlers begin to grow after the old ones are cast in April. They are regrown and cleaned of velvet by the rutting season, often rubbing it off on a holly bush as it dries. Each year's antler growth gives the buck a name. A yearling is a pricket, one of two years a sorel, which in turn is followed by a sore, a bare buck, a buck, and a great buck.

Right A Fallow doe on the alert. They rely greatly on receiving and leaving scents, and will often stand and watch someone approaching, only finally disappearing when they pick up a scent. The natural camouflage of their coats and their ability to remain motionless makes them easy to miss in woodland.

Left Fallow Deer fawns when about two months old.

Below Sika deer hinds, a 19th century importation from the Orient. There are about 100 in the New Forest, and all are successors of a small band that escaped from the Beaulieu Estate at the turn of the century. Coming from a warmer climate, they are said in the New Forest never to go north of the railway. The word 'sika' means deer, so - as a Japanese-speaking friend commented - if you say 'Sika deer', you're saying 'deer deer'. They are about the same height as a fallow, but have a much heavier appearance.

A roebuck feeding at dawn on the edge of the woodland. Unlike the fallow and red deer, who live mostly in herds of separate sexes, the delicate little roe stays with his own small family. He stakes out a territory in the woods, marking it with scent and by bashing his antlers on the bushes. They are mainly active at night, eating grass and berries, or browsing on the leaves of oak, bramble and birch - as in this photograph. Roe deer only became firmly established in the Forest in the 1920s, and they now number about 300.

Keepers building a High Seat. Elevated platforms like this one lift the observer above the animals' scent and its habitual eyeline. The High Seats are usually built on the edge of a wood overlooking an open area where deer often feed.

Lunchtime at the Forestry Commission Deer Sanctuary at Boldrewood. The practice of feeding the deer started in the severe winter of 1962/63, initially with potatoes. It now goes on throughout the year - except at rutting-time - and visitors can watch them eating grain scattered by the keepers. Note that there are no does, the bucks keep them away!

KINGS AND COMMONERS

KINGS AND COMMONERS

In the middle of the area chosen for the new royal forest was a cross-roads of tracks – east to west from Southampton Water to the River Avon; south to north from the seashore up to where the chalk hills begin to rise. It divided the area almost exactly into quarters and was called Lyndhurst, the 'Wood of the Lime Trees', which were once plentiful but are now rare in the Forest.

Lyndhurst was already a royal manor in Saxon times, and we know for certain that from the outset the Normans chose it as the headquarters of their New Forest. One proof of this lies in the existence, still visible today, of a great bank in the shape of a giant funnel around Lyndhurst. On top of it there would have been a high fence of split oak that raised the corral to a deer-proof height. When in use, the mouth of the funnel was extended for long distances with 'sewilling' – cords stretched on short stakes and dressed all along with turkey and goose feathers. Thus large quantities of deer could be quietly steered into the Old Park corral and held for royal use.

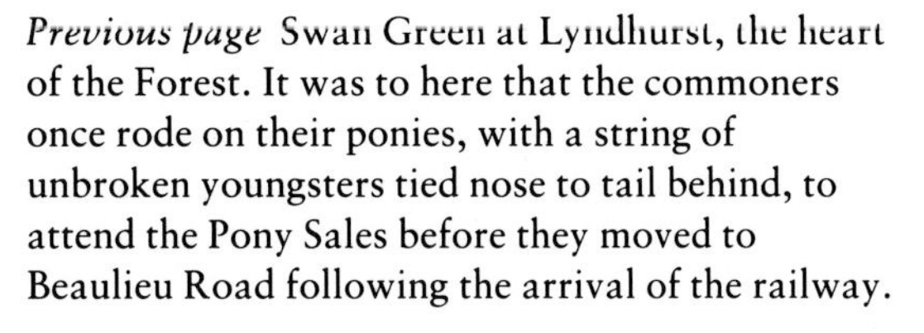

Previous page Swan Green at Lyndhurst, the heart of the Forest. It was to here that the commoners once rode on their ponies, with a string of unbroken youngsters tied nose to tail behind, to attend the Pony Sales before they moved to Beaulieu Road following the arrival of the railway.

Bolton's Bench, Lyndhurst, on a typical Bank Holiday weekend. To be precise, Bolton's Bench is actually the high ground behind the ice-cream van, and owes its name to a large natural knoll, sometimes thought to be an ancient burial mound, and Lord Bolton, Lord Warden of the Forest in 1688. Lyndhurst is the 'capital' of the Forest and the only town of any size inside the Perambulation, or official boundary. In the background can be seen the spire of the church of St Michael, built from 1858-1870 and described by John Betjeman as the most 'fanciful, fantastic Gothic style I have ever seen.'

Visitors looking at the Rufus Stone in Canterton Glen. Here, or hereabouts - for no one is certain, a wood-gatherer called Purkess found the body of William II in August 1100, after he had been slain by Sir Walter Tyrrell with an arrow (both Purkess and Tyrrell are still common names in the New Forest). William Rufus was a ruthless and unpopular monarch, and it now seems probable that there was a conspiracy to murder him. The Stone was erected in 1745 by Lord Delaware, Master Keeper at Bolderwood Lodge, but was so defaced by relic-hunters that it was encased in iron in 1841.

So it was at Lyndhurst that the King's House was built from which to govern the Forest, or the Queen's House as it has always been called when a woman occupies the throne. From here has always been managed this last piece in the great jigsaw created by the Saxon Kings. The size of the whole enterprise is difficult to imagine. Within a generation, King John had at his disposal sixty-eight Forests, thirteen Chases where he shared the deer-rights with the aristocracy, and seventy-eight Parks where smaller herds could be kept enclosed. A great machine for the supply of fresh meat controlled from the royal household by the Surveyor of Forests.

Co-existing side by side with the administration of the Royal Forest were the rights enjoyed – and jealously guarded – by the commoners. These rights were being exercised long before William established the Forest, when waste and uncultivated land was held in common for use by all. There are a series of books kept at Lyndhurst called the 'Atlas' which list the six everyday rights of the commoners: the right to graze cattle and ponies (pasture), to dig turf and gather firewood (turbary and estovers), the right to keep sheep (overy), to turn out pigs to forage on acorns (mast), and the right to dig for lime-rich clay for use as a fertilizer (marl). The importance of the deer to the medieval kings, followed by the gradual increase in the need for timber, has often led to friction between the Crown and the commoners. More recently their contribution to the way of life in the Forest has been better understood. Today, their ponies and livestock graze nearly 45,000 acres of unenclosed land. It is a unique and ancient system of agriculture, and one which has done much to create and preserve the traditional character of the Forest.

Far left Queen's House, Lyndhurst, the 'seat' of government of the Forest. The first probable mention of a building on the site dates to 1297, when twenty oaks were felled 'to make laths for the Queen's manor house at Lyndhurst'. The queen in question was Eleanor of Castile, wife of Edward I, who lived in Lyndhurst whilst her husband was away fighting the Welsh. The building was enlarged during the Tudor period, and rebuilt in brick by Charles I and Charles II, probably as a royal hunting lodge. For a while it was the official residence of the Deputy Surveyor, but was handed over to the Forestry Commission when they took over the management of the Forest in 1924.

Left The Agisters outside the Verderers' Court, from left to right: Raymond Bennett, Jonathan Garrelli, Andrew Napthine, John Booth, and the Head Agister, Brian Ingram. They wear their green jackets, breeches, leather gaiters and hard hats bearing the insignia of the Verderers' Stirrup at all sittings of the Court of Verderers, as well as other special occasions. The Agisters are usually recruited from amongst the commoners, and are responsible for the commoners livestock. They deal with the inevitable casualties caused by road accidents, collect the grazing fees, brand and tail-mark the ponies after the autumn round-up, and keep a watch on the condition of the stock on their beat.

Left The Verderers' Hall, Queen's House, Lyndhurst. The Forest laws were originally upheld by a whole range of courts, but the only one to survive is the Court of Swainmote and Attachment, better known as the Verderers' Court. Its main purpose is to safeguard the interests of the commoners. It meets in open court every second month, and the commoners still exercise their ancient right of 'presentment' by bringing before the ten Verderers sitting at the high bench any matter that concerns them. The Royal Arms above the bench commemorate the last visit of the Justice in Eyre in 1669.

Above Commoners' cattle drinking in the watersplash at Brockenhurst. The Forest cottagers have always lived on close terms with their livestock. 'Incomers', moving in more recently, have often found it odd to open their front door and meet the backside of a four-footed neighbour.

Above right Ted Penny turning hay at Emery Down, on land enclosed by commoners at some time in the past. Penny is a well-known Forest name. Ted runs a smallholding of his own and helps other commoners during haymaking.

Right Forester Peter Brown BEM splitting sweet chestnut for fencing in Hasley Inclosure, where sweet chestnut is still coppiced. Very few craftsmen still retain the traditional forestry skills, but I have seen a commoner make a superb five-bar fieldgate from boles, using only a felling axe and a broken table-knife.

The Common of Pasture, one of the six traditional commoners' rights, here seen being enjoyed by both cattle and ponies in Latchmore Bottom. The commoners' livestock are the architects of this open Forest landscape, and without being grazed in the traditional way much of the Forest would revert to thick woodland.

Right The Common of Turbary. This inn sign hangs appropriately at East Boldre. On one side lies the flat peaty heathland of the sort where turves were cut, on the other the longest line of small forest-edge holdings. Here the turf fuel maintained the cottagers' fires, with the aid of a few faggots and bits of stump wood.

The Common of Mast, young pigs feeding on acorns near Denny. The sixty day period when pigs were traditionally turned out is known as the pannage season and used to start on September 25th, but now both its start and length are dictated by the size of the acorn crop and the dates decided by the Forestry Commission and Verderers. The Common is an important one, for acorns are poisonous to ponies, and the pigs appetite for them keeps down the number of ponies who die from acorn poisoning.

The Common of Fuelwood, or Estovers, means the entitlement to wood for fuel. It originally meant dead trees and broken branches, but nowadays the timber is provided by the Forestry Commission from commercial felling in the inclosures. Only a few commoners have the right to Estovers, which is now cut in four feet lengths and supplied as stacks four feet wide by eight feet long, known as a cord. Each 1 ½ ton cord is numbered, and in early autumn the commoners entitled to fuelwood are told the number of their cord and where to find it.

Commoners' stock, part of a small herd of Highlanders. The favourite Forest milk-cow was the Brindle, a black-streaked Jersey cross. They rarely strayed far, but wore a plate-iron cowbell, and the old women went out to milk them carrying a milking stool and bucket.

Cattle drinking in Ober Water, near Brockenhurst. There are now just over 2,200 cattle in the Forest, and the numbers are rising.

THE FOREST RIVERS AN
THE SOUTHERN SHORE

THE FOREST RIVERS AND THE SOUTHERN SHORE

A friend of mine said that if you know a countryside you should be able to look over any little bridge down any little lane and tell where the water flowing below will reach the sea. A good point – flowing water makes a great contribution to the patterns of geography.

It is easy to get a picture of the New Forest waterways into your mind. To the north a few streams run east and west to the Forest boundaries – into the River Test and thus to Southampton Water; into the River Avon and on to join the Dorset Stour and empty into the sea at Christchurch.

Through the main part of the Forest – shelving regularly to the Solent coast – run many little streams with pretty names: Ober Water, Highland Water, Dockens Water, Silver Stream. Wandering south through the woodland they join together to form three small rivers – Beaulieu River, Lymington River and the Avon Water. Each of these has had an impact on Forest history.

Wherever the streams are impeded they spread and deposit nutrients that become small green feeding places. Lower down they flood widely and, with help from grazing stock, create the famous streamside 'lawns' that are the joy of children and the commoners' animals. The whole system ends in three tidal estuaries, patterned with quiet creeks and surrounded by the saltmarshes, throughout time the home of the sea-birds.

From the beginning these three places have been important to man. Lymington soon became the Forest port; in fact when the Conqueror's son Rufus was assassinated while deer-hunting the supposed murderer, Sir Walter Tyrrell, was able to take ship to France from Lymington on the evening of the crime. Later, when the King added the export of salt to his Forest enterprises, Lymington exported it to many countries. Now that the sheltered Solent has become the greatest of sailing centres, it has become a place of yacht clubs, marinas and boat-builders.

At the mouth of the eastern river King John, seeking forgiveness of his sins, gave a wide stretch of land to some Cistercian monks from Normandy. They sailed up the estuary with great barges of their native stone and built a grand abbey. They called their extensive, self-sufficient enterprise Bellus Locus, which when translated from Latin into Norman-French became Beaulieu – or 'lovely place'.

To the west the Avon Water slipped out of the Forest, through the widest of the salt-marshes to the great Hurst shingle-bank. Here the fishing boats lay, the wildfowlers set their nets and the commoners collected gulls' eggs which found their way as a luxury as far as London. Here also Henry VIII mounted coastal guns at Hurst Castle.

Previous page A winter stream in full flow running past a stool of alder, once in demand for fine charcoal and clog-making, with the Hard Fern, which likes to live close to it. These winter torrents carry down silt, impoverishing the upper land but enriching the alluvial grazings below.

Latchmore Stream, which rises in the north of the Forest in Islands Thorn Inclosure and wanders gently through marshes and over flood-washed gravels and grazing lawns. Here it passes through Amberwood Inclosure, as shown by the bluebells, which do not thrive in places where the Forest is grazed.

Winter flooding at Longwater Lawn on the Beaulieu River. Compare this with the same area of lawn in high summer on the opposite page. These upper waters of the Beaulieu River are the spawning grounds of the fine sea-trout that annually run up-stream. Often easy to see, they are exceedingly hard to catch – even by those who have the rights to fish for them.

Water Crowfoot flowering in the Beaulieu River at Longwater Lawn.

Left Shepton Water at Pig Bush Passage, where the ford has been replaced by a bridge, before flowing east into the Beaulieu River.

Palace House, Beaulieu, the first great house to be built in the Forest. The house was converted from the 14th century Abbey gatehouse following the dissolution of the Abbey in 1538 by Thomas Wriothesley, later Earl of Southampton, and founder of the Montagu family.

The Beaulieu River near Exbury.

The Kingfisher knows every stream in the New Forest and patrols them with his characteristic level straight-line flight. Their diet consists mainly of minnows and sticklebacks, also water-beetles and dragonfly nymphs, and they beat their catch on a branch before bolting it down, head first.

Beaulieu Mill Pond at dawn in May. This beautiful pond was originally created during the reign of King John by a dam so as to drive the wheel of a corn-mill. It is now the roost of a dozen species of wildfowl.

Beaulieu tide-mill and pond. Just below the mill, where the freshwater joins the estuary, the medieval monks threw their seine nets on the rising tide to catch their Friday fish. Not so long ago I saw the net drawn by the estate fisherman, with her Ladyship choosing the fish for Palace House before the villagers took their share.

Buckler's Hard below a threatening sky, with one of the two rows of houses that face one-another across the main street. The Hard was originally conceived by the 2nd Duke of Montagu as a port for importing sugar in the early eighteenth century. The venture failed, partly because an expedition to found an estate in the West Indies was driven off by pirates. It later became a shipbuilding yard, and nearly seventy vessels were launched from its slips into the Beaulieu River between 1745 and 1818, including one of Nelson's favourite warships, the 64 gun *Agammemnon*. As well as the fascinating Maritime Museum, one house is furnished as a shipwright's cottage of the 1790s, whilst the old Master Shipbuilder's house is now a hotel.

Downstream of the old landing-place at Buckler's Hard on the Beaulieu River.

Opposite page The Lymington River in autumn. A network of streams in the centre of the Forest gather together north of Brockenhurst to form the river, which runs down past the Iron Age hillfort of Buckland Rings – where Roman galleys once landed – on through beds of thatching reed before reaching the Forest's main harbour.

SU 2
SOUTHAMPTON
SNOWFLAKE

Lymington Harbour. In summer, the water around the Royal Lymington Yacht Club, from which the Princess Royal sails, and the old Town Yacht Club is a forest of masts, such is the town's popularity as a yachting centre.

A Wightlink ferry leaving Lymington for Yarmouth on the Isle of Wight. Lymington was founded in about 1200 as a new town because of its closeness to the Isle of Wight, and the earliest ferries were flat-bottomed hoys (hence 'ship ahoy') that daily crossed over to Yarmouth laden with livestock and goods. The ferries that plied to and fro during the 1930s were built in Germany and, I am told, when one of them broke down during the War the builders obligingly smuggled over spares through neutral Portugal.

Above The church of St Thomas, Lymington, with its lovely 18th century cupola. Henry Lyte (1793-1847) was once curate, and whilst in Lymington wrote many famous hymns, including 'Praise my soul, the King of Heaven' and 'Abide with me'.

Above right Captains Row, Lymington. I was once told by a retired policeman that in the old days, particularly when a coal boat was in or the fishing fleet couldn't sail because of bad weather, that no one ventured down Captains Row except in pairs because the area of the town near the quay was so rough.

Right Quay Hill, Lymington, and now a mixture of nautical shops, boutiques and restaurants. The building at the bottom was built in about 1700 as a house, but eventually became the Solent Inn, and for a long time brewed its own beer.

The remains of the old salt pans west of Lymington, the basis of its prosperity in the Middle Ages and once a conspicuous feature of the marshes between Pylewell and Hurst. The pans were shallow twenty yard square pools edged with mudbanks. Seawater was taken from ponds that had trapped seawater at high tide using wooden balers and placed in the pans, where it was left to evaporate. Small windmills constantly pumped the evaporating water from pan to pan until it became brine, after which it was channelled into the boiling houses, where furnaces boiled the brine till it became salt. The industry was at its height in the mid-eighteenth century when 163 pans were in operation. The introduction of Cheshire salt in 1865 made sea-salt uneconomic, and the marshes were gradually levelled and turned into grazing grounds.

The Solent near Pitts Deep. For a short distance between the old quay at Pitts Deep and the mouth of the Beaulieu River the original New Forest boundary touches the sea. I have been out here with old foresters wading chest-deep with six foot shrimp nets – and returned home with a gallon for tea.

First light on the Avon Water, which rises in Holmsley Bog south of Burley and reaches the sea at Keyhaven.

Looking out over the marshes at Keyhaven towards Hurst Castle and Lighthouse. The marshes support a major colony of Black-headed Gulls. The locals once mercilessly raided their nests, as their eggs are a gourmet delicacy, but now the taking is strictly controlled. Next door to the Gun Inn is Hawker's cottage, the retreat of Colonel Peter Hawker (1786-1853), the great wildfowler who could be called the Isaak Walton of shooting. From here he took his great punt-gun (now a museum piece) out through the creeks. The High Lighthouse on Hurst Spit was built in 1867, but the Castle dates back to the 1540s, when it was built by Henry VIII as a defensive fort – largely with stone from Beaulieu Abbey.

The old and the new on opposing tacks off the Forest shore. A modern yacht and an old gaff-rigged smack pass one-another in a north-westerly breeze. Behind rise the chalk hills of the Isle of Wight.

FOREST PONIES

FOREST PONIES

For a start, there are no wild ponies in the New Forest. A charter of Henry II speaks of 'wild horses', and perhaps then there may have been some who had escaped domestication. Long before that most of the native stock had entered partnership with the native people. Queen Bodicea, after all, used four of them to pull her chariot.

What you see here are ranched ponies living and feeding on the range – rounded up, coralled and marked with the brands of commoners with the right to pasture. For strength and hardihood, courage and intelligence they are remarkable. Let me present one of them as an example of the breed. He was born on the Forest out of a strawberry mare belonging to Bob House of Monkshorn. He grew to be a bright bay, thirteen and a half hands high. His name was Johnny. In 1954 the Pony Society chose him as their Personality of the Year:

"He worked all the year round on the farm, ploughing, pulling logs, harrowing and carting hay, and he was a perfect driving pony. He loved children and gave great courage to the ones he taught to ride. But he could carry a grown man and hunted many days with the Portman, jumping higher than himself and often giving the hunters a lead over tricky fences. When polo came to Rhinefield he took to the game without training. He showed his stamina by coming first three times running in the Open Point-to-Point and his speed by several times winning the Burley Scurry. At the age of sixteen he still seemed to get younger every day."

Great trouble is taken to preserve the breed of ponies like Johnny. Only stallions of the highest quality can be turned out on the Forest. Every year they are judged and chosen by the Verderers, and then each is taken to his own district where he can gather a party of mares. Thus each commoner can take his mares to the sire of his choice.

The foals are born in the quiet of the woods and, when they are well on their feet, brought to join the others on the open grazing. There can hardly be a prettier sight than Balmer Lawn when half a hundred mares have assembled there with their foals.

New Forest ponies are of many colours, reflecting the earlier years when people brought other breeds to the Forest, thinking to 'improve'. Queen Victoria once even sent down an Arab stallion. They will grow to different sizes and various types, even since the Pony Society was founded to guard the breed. In recent years I have still heard heated disagreements between pony people, some arguing for the old working sort with its biggish head, generous bone and the 'hard palate' that enabled it to graze gorse and holly; others wanting more 'style' to match the export market for smart children's ponies that had a boom in recent years.

For myself, I think they should breed them all as near as they can get to old Johnny.

Previous page Mare and foal.

Ponies on the edge of Brinken Wood in the cold of winter. Although in the depths of winter ponies may have to eat moss, twigs and holly, it was surviving the tough times that gave the native breeds their hardiness – a quality they would soon lose with too much pampering. Throughout the winter a watch is kept on the ponies by the Agisters – the mounted servants of the Court of Verderers – who can recognize an animal's condition, even through a long winter coat. They have the power to order an ailing pony to be taken back to the homestead for extra feeding.

A 'party' of ponies grazing the lawns beside the Avon Water. In the spring the chosen stallions are farmed out, each in his territory, where a group of mares gathers with him. Although the sire may sometimes move the mares to keep them together and away from another male, it is always an older mare who holds the leadership of the group.

Ponies at shade in Latchmore Bottom. When the flies are at their worst the ponies stand and doze at chosen places throughout the Forest. Many of their shading places have remained unaltered within living memory. I believe them to be places where the natural lie of the land causes thermals, which lift the flies up out of reach away from the ponies. Shade places also exist on roads that were once tracks, and motorists are often taken aback by meeting a mob of dozing ponies in the road that show no inclination to move.

Ponies grazing in the open woods. At foaling time the mare drives away last year's youngster, if it is still following her, and retires to woodland cover. In a short time the new-born foal is up on its feet and moving. The yearling may then rejoin them, and they set off for the grazings.

Below Ponies shading under a 'creep' beneath the A35. New Forest ponies do not seem to fear traffic in the way that other horses do, with the result that each year many are killed on the unfenced roads. A foal can cross unexpectedly to join its mother, and the visitors habit of feeding the ponies – though asked not to do so – helps attract them to the roadside.

Driving ponies to holding pens during the annual drift, or round up. The drifts take place throughout the autumn to take account of the differing ages of the foals and are times of great excitement in the Forest. The Forest is divided into areas, with the agister for each organizing the drift with the help of other riders. Drift days are when the commoners' children who ride really learn to stay in the saddle going fast across rough country.

Drift ponies in the pound, waiting to be tail-marked and branded by the agister. The tails are cut into one of four patterns, depending on the area, so that animals belonging to each district can be recognized at a distance. In the foreground is the fire used to heat the branding-irons used to brand the foals with their owner's particular mark. This is increasingly being replaced by a process of freeze-branding for which the same brand marks can be used.

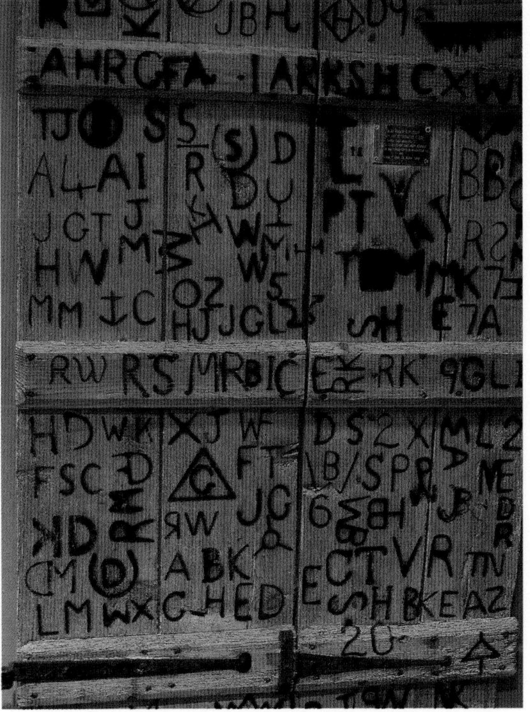

A grey foal in the auction ring at Beaulieu Road during one of the five annual sales. The last is usually the biggest, with up to five hundred ponies passing through the ring. The popularity of the New Forester as a child's pony has greatly increased since the 2nd World War. Prior to that – old commoners tell me – seventy per cent were sold into working harness – builders and bakers' carts, or down the mines as pit ponies.

A selection of commoners' brands.

A pony on Longwater Lawn.

Ponies in Hatchet Pond in the heat of the summer. On hot days, the ponies paddle deep into the mires and ponds, even feeding on water-plants. The Forest streams are also as much an attraction to them as they are to the visitors' children.

A pony and trap in Bratley Wood, or the older way to travel. For centuries, the ponies were the only power available to forest-dwellers. They worked on the smallholdings, galloped under the saddle, and drove to market and to church. But there are many for whom harness-driving remains a passionate hobby. I remember the Queen buying herself a pair from a member of the New Forest Pony Society.

THE HEATHLANDS

THE HEATHLANDS

Travelling west along the main road to Ringwood or Fordingbridge, you see the New Forest as a great heathland. A sweeping landscape – awe-inspiring in some weathers – of heather, gorse and bracken, criss-crossed by gravel tracks that seem to reveal the bones of the earth. Altogether the 30,000 acres of heathland in the Forest form what is the largest area of heath in Europe.

Not long ago it reached across the River Avon to run right on down to the sea beyond Poole. But that Dorset heathland – Hardy's Egdon Heath – has now been largely developed out of existence. Now people say, "Stop! Enough! No more destruction of the native heath by Man!" Yet there is strong evidence that it was man who first created it.

Early settlers would have come down from the north, from the densely-populated chalk, bringing with them their primitive agricultural methods. From patch to patch they went – cutting, burning and moving on as each plot lost its fertility. As the ground was laid bare, the rain washed the life out of the poorer soil. In many places underneath the heath lie traces of the primary forest, the Greenwood, sometimes in a state of partial clearance.

Later it was to the open spaces that the commoners brought their turf spades, seeking fuel for their home fires. When I bought a ruined farmhouse the windows in the back wall were within five inches of the ground, with clumsy steps down to the back door. "That," said an old lady, "is where they put the turf. There was always a bit left each year when the next lot was chucked in." Records show that each year up to three million turves were cut, and that – cutting one and leaving two – could damage up to a hundred acres of ground.

When their day came the commoners continued burning the heathland. It was claimed as a method of improving stock grazing but, more than incidentally, it prevented the Greenwood from growing back into the heath area.

In the end the Crown took it over in order to control it and nowadays in the winter you can still watch the controlled burnings – a large area each year, but in small patches spread apart in order not to break up natural habitats.

So was this heathland a primary feature of lowland Britain? Or does it owe its character to man and the ways in which he has used it over the centuries?

Certainly it is nowadays held precious for its wildlife, the many rare species for which it provides a home. The Wild Gladiolus that blooms in the shade of the bracken, the Dartford Warbler that finds winter insect food under the heather. The Hobby hunts, the Smooth Snake slips by and the Sand Lizard sits in the sun. The Nightjar purrs in the dark and here until recently (and hopefully soon again) lived the Red-Backed Shrike and the Natterjack Toad.

Previous page The flower of the bracken. The very rare Wild Gladiolus only lives in the New Forest, and even then it was not discovered until 1856. The decline of bracken-cutting has probably helped it to survive.

A Dartford Warbler in February, looking forward to the spring. A non-migrating insect-eater, in hard winters the Dartford Warbler takes refuge deep in the heather and gorse, where it can still find food. The old commoners were unfamiliar with its name (it was christened in Kent) and often called it the Fuzz Acker – a name it often shared with the Stonechat. It remains one of our rarest birds, and the hard winter of 1962-63 reduced the entire British population to about ten pairs.

Left The Heath Spotted Orchid. Of nearly fifty British orchids this is the one that belongs specially to the heathlands; and its presence is a sign of acid soil. As with other orchids, the minute seeds grow so slowly that sometimes the first leaves may not appear for three years, and the first flower up to ten.

Below left The Bee Orchid, in flower in July.

Below The Silver Studded Blue, one of the commonest butterflies of the New Forest heaths and easily spotted in high summer.

Looking across Cunninger Bottom in April. Much of the heath was once wooded forest, but over the last five thousand years rain has gradually washed the soil and nutrients out of the gravel terraces and down to the lower lands. Early man accelerated the change by using fire to clear the land for farming, and subsequent grazing by both the deer and the commoners' stock has helped to maintain its character. The heaths can be a grim place in hard winters, but they have great grandeur and support a fascinating natural history, including some very rare species.

An adder, or viper, our only native poisonous snake. As well as the adder, the much rarer smooth snake also lives on the heath. The adder grows to about two feet long, and is recognized by the distinctive zig-zag down its back. It can detect someone approaching from a long distance, and will then move away – for it is not aggressive.

The smooth snake is longer and slimmer than the adder. It almost always stays close to water, taking frequent baths to cool itself.

Cranesmoor from Castle Hill. Although the bracken is not very appetising at first glance it has always been an important 'feed' and New Forest ponies could work hard on a 'fuzz' diet. Commoners once cut the younger shoots with a special 'fuzz' hook, and it was then chopped in a chaff-cutter.

A sand lizard, a true heathland rarity which only lives on these southern heaths and a few sand dunes in the north of England, and is recognized by the sprinkle of white dots along its dark back. It lives communally, and feeds on insects, including butterflies. In winter they hibernate using holes left by mice and voles, despite being capable of digging their own tunnels. They also retire below ground in summer when the sun gets too hot, and in attempts to escape heathland fires.

Stephill Bottom from Fernycrofts on a late afternoon in February, usually the hardest month. The snakes hibernate, the Dartford Warbler hides deep in the heather, but somewhere in the mist the ponies still browse, and the solitary Scots pine still stands where it isn't wanted.

Wilverley, and high summer on the heath. The purple heather contrasts with the green of bracken and gorse. All three are valuable in Forest agriculture, but here you can also see the most disliked tree of all, the self-sown Scots pine. Each of them will drop a crop of cones, establishing a new area of pines and blanking out the grazing with a thick carpet of needles and dead cones.

Above Controlled heath-burning near Castle Hill. After a great deal of casual burning by commoners in past times, burning is now controlled and strictly managed as a way of clearing the heath of scrub and encouraging new growth of bracken and gorse. The work is done by the Forestry Commission between October and the end of March, with the aim of burning about fifteen hundred acres a year, or five per cent of the total heathland.

Left Yew Tree Heath ten years after an accidental summer fire, with the yellow of mosses and lichens. The controlled winter 'burns' do not kill the roots and seeds, only the tops, whereas summer fires completely sterilise the soil and can burn down deep into the peat.

Right The woodland creeps back. Without being grazed by ponies and stock the heath would revert to scrub – as here near Halfpenny Green.

A mare and foal near Pitt's Wood. Bracken was the commoners' straw, and used to be cut, dried and carted back to the holdings in the autumn for use as winter bedding. There is no doubt that by abandoning the cutting of fern the commoners have significantly reduced their area of grazing.

THE WETLANDS

THE WETLANDS

From the time the Dutch came over to dig the great drains in East Anglia during the seventeeth century to the steam-driven cable rigs of my youth, followed by the invention of the long-arm mechanical digger, farmers have struggled to make the water run speedily off the land. By their efforts they ultimately produced the most efficient agriculture in the world; but also caused discontent among conservationists who mourn the disappearance of 'wetland' habitat.

Consequently the numerous small bogs of the New Forest are beloved by naturalists. The valley bogs in the Forest cover 7,000 acres, an area greater than all the other bogs in England combined. In the north of the Forest they were formed by slow seepage out between the layers of soil exposed on the slopes, in the south in hollows on flatter land. They are known as the 'mires' and each of them supports up to a hundred plant species, including such rarities as the Slender Cotton Grass and the Giant Sundew. Three-quarters of Britain's dragonfly species live on them. They are beloved by the wader birds that come for their courtship, shuttling back to the Solent shore to feed.

Previous page The Forest mires. All over the Forest, where the slope is slight and the bottom impenetrable, you will find boggy patches – as here near Pig Bush. Commoners once gathered the sphagnum moss in the peaty bottoms to sell to florists, now it can be taken only by license. Some mires are home to more than a hundred species of water-loving plants, and they in turn form a reservoir of moisture that feeds the Forest streams even in the heat of summer.

The Forest ponds have a special beauty. This is Long Pond on the road from Burley, where the ponies stand up to their ribs in water in high summer and splash their tails as they nibble at the water-plants.

Hatchet Pond on the eastern edge of Beaulieu Heath, the angler's favourite Forest pond and for which day tickets can be bought. It was made by linking a row of disused marl pits and its waters once drove a hammer-mill for ironworkers in East Boldre.

The mires hold water all summer and many of the small Forest streams would dry in the hot season but for the water fed to them from these reservoirs. In their hearts many commoners would like to see them drained in order to extend the grazing for stock. It has been a recurring subject of contention. But some places that were claimed to have been inundated within recent memory have been proved to have peat bottoms that started gathering more than five thousand years ago.

Anyhow, through the ages the commoners themselves have turned many Forest sites from land to water. There are more than three hundred ponds in the Forest, some formed out of old gravel and clay pits, but many more created by the digging of marl.

In the days before manufacturing chemistry and the advance of heavy transport marl was the only dressing that could be put on the land to improve the poor soil. It is a form of limey clay that crops up in particular places. The Normans granted rights for marl pits and it was carted until the early days of Queen Victoria.

Now these many ponds have had time to grow a natural mantle of shrubs and reeds and water-plants, including the rare Water Violet. They have become places of beauty and the resort of fishermen. Hatchet Pond, perhaps the anglers' favourite, was formed by linking together a group of marl pits.

There are also small cob-ponds that provided the material for the local houses. Waters were created by the nobility as wildfowl decoys, including the great Bishop's Dyke. And down at Beaulieu the river waters were gathered into a mill pool to work the wheel of the old mill first built by the monks.

Canada geese on Eyeworth Pond. Not many years ago the first pair of Canada geese came to the saltings at Beaulieu. They prospered enormously, and before I left Monkshorn Farm I counted a flock of eighty feeding on the newly-cut barley stubble. Eyeworth Pond was originally created to provide water for a gunpowder mill at Eyeworth Lodge.

The common frog at spawning time – but unfortunately not anything like as common as he used to be.

The curlew lives between the heath and the shore. In winter, his long beak probes the mud on the salt marshes, whilst in summer he breeds on the heath. The call of the curlew is unmistakable, and exactly matches his name.

The snipe, best known of the wetland birds. Throughout history his zig-zag flight has defeated all but the best shots. In summer he announces himself with his 'drumming', a deep fluttering noise caused by his tail feathers that can be heard as he dives over his territory.

The birth of a dragonfly. The Southern Hawker climbs from the shuck of the larva, which before crawling up a plant stem spent its life underwater, to become a perfect mature dragonfly. Twenty-nine of the forty to fifty species of dragonfly that exist in Britain find a home on the ponds and mires of the New Forest – and for some it may be their last refuge.

Left Sowley Pond, the largest stretch of fresh water in the Forest. It lies between the Forest and the Solent shore and was once part of the Beaulieu Abbey estate. In the autumn I have found it to provide glorious pike-fishing, and in winter it is a wonderful place to watch wildfowl. The medieval fish pond was extended in about 1600 to create sufficient water to operate an ironworks tilt hammer. The furnaces were fed with Forest timber, and the ironstone was collected on the coast.

Right The causeway leading into the great beechwood at Woodfidley, which used to be known as the place where the most rain fell in the Forest. True or not, it is certainly bordered by boggy areas, over which this causeway was built so that commoners and animals could pass in safety.

Below Fishing at Cadman's Pool. The pool is one of a series dug by Arthur Cadman, the great deer expert, when he was Deputy Surveyor in places where he thought they were scarce, and this one is named after him.

The boundary of Bishop's Dyke, once a great decoy pond but now an open low-lying boggy waste. According to legend, a medieval Bishop of Winchester is supposed to have asked the king for land in the Forest. The king had little liking for the bishop, who was enormously fat, and told him that he could have all the land he could crawl around without stopping. Not to be outwitted, the bishop had built a flat trolley with large wheels on which he could rest his belly on – and he ended up with Bishop's Dyke.

The Marsh Gentian. Although the damp heath habitat it favours is on the decline throughout Britain, this flower – beloved of bumble-bees – is safe in the wet places of the New Forest.

FOREST ROOFS

FOREST ROOFS

The New Forest would appear at first sight to have not much architectural distinction. Yet its history is visible to anyone who looks at its buildings with an inquisitive eye.

At the start, apart from the administrative buildings at Lyndhurst, the Kings ordered hunting-lodges to be built – like Castle Malwood where Rufus was staying at the time of his death. And early documents order houses to be built in lonely places for the Keepers – each in charge of his Walk.

Meanwhile the commoners' homes were primitive – pole-huts, like the one made famous in the picture of Brusher Mills, built surreptitiously and guarded in secrecy or through bribery until residence was established. Then everywhere they built the cob-houses with walls of pummelled clay and gravel reinforced with heather faggots. I knew many of these, but do not now know one in its original form. At Furzey Lodge, where the Kitcher family cob dwellings were faced with brick a generation ago, a single ruined cob cottage lies empty.

In contrast to this simplicity were the great buildings of Beaulieu Abbey. When the monks were turned out the Gatehouse was converted into Palace House, the home of the

Previous page I make no apology for including this old but historic picture of Brusher Mills in the book, for as well as being one of the most famous images of the Forest it gives a glimpse of its earliest dwellings – the pole shelter. Brusher was a snake-catcher, and is supposed to have caught more than three thousand adders in fourteen years, selling some to zoos, and the fat of others as a medicine. He spent thirty years in his hut at Queen's Bower and is thought to owe his nickname to brushing Lyndhurst cricket pitch between innings. But the word is much older in the Forest, for 'brushers' were those who went out in the winter with 'brush- hooks' to cut down branches for the stock to browse on.

Monkshorn Farmhouse on the Beaulieu Rails, and my home for many years. Beaulieu Rails is the 11th century bank that bounded the Abbey estate, and the house was first built by the monks, probably for a senior lay-brother who supervised this part of their lands. It can be no coincidence that for many centuries it was lived in by a family called House. Left derelict by a later change of boundaries, I restored it as accurately as possible – apart from the conversion of a calf shed into a kitchen.

A brick and tile cottage at Bank. The Forest small-holdings have always been essential to the wide open grazing by commoners' stock. At Bank such holdings were gathered round the Eyre estate – a name surely descended from the Justices in Eyre who periodically visited the New Forest to try cases in its courts during the Middle Ages.

Montagu family today. Part of the stone was sold, some of it to build Calshot Castle and the early Hurst Castle. When we came to Monkshorn we found the well was of abbey stone and in the garden was a holy-water stoop used to feed the chickens.

It was William Gilpin, Vicar of Boldre, who first wrote romantically about the Forest, and started a fashion that encouraged the well-to-do down to visit the Forest armed with sketch-books. Some settled, leaving behind here and there some fanciful and picturesque cottages.

On the few remaining estates where farmhouses were still tenanted, the landlords took advantage of the new railway to bring down Midland brick and Welsh tiles for rebuilding them. Our second house in the Forest was one of these on the old Compton manor, and behind it lay the ruins of the older cob buildings, now overgrown by a forest of elder trees.

In later Victorian times arose a few mansions. Lord Harcourt, the Prime Minister, built himself one on the foundations of Rufus's Castle Malwood, whilst the ultra-Victorian Rhinefield House, with its avenue of ornamental trees, is now a hotel.

Through it all have survived some fine churches. St. John's at Boldre, where the old vicarage is now called Gilpins. St. Thomas's at Lymington with a lovely Georgian interior, where Mr. Lyle, the curate, wrote the hymn 'Abide with Me'. All Saints at Minstead where an extra gallery was built to accommodate more worshippers, and the three tier pulpit allowed for preaching at different levels.

Arthur Conan Doyle, who gave us Sherlock Holmes, worshipped and was buried here. From here too he went to Beaulieu to investigate the doings of Mrs. 'Witchy' White and to lie in wait at night for the spirits of long-dead monks.

The Abbey remains, Beaulieu. The Cistercian Abbey was founded by King John as a penance in 1204, who also gave the monks land and exemption from toll and taxes. Following its dissolution in 1538 the refectory (on the right) became the parish church. Also visible are part of the cloisters.

Beaulieu High Street. The Cistercian monks operated a brick and tile yard, founding a style for the buildings on their estate which is still recognizable today.

A nineteenth century keeper's cottage near Vinney Ridge, complete with a set of antlers either side of the window. An early order commanded lodges to be built for the keepers in the remotest places possible, surrounded by bank and hedge, so that each could keep watch over his 'walk'.

Rhinefield House, the last great house to be built in the Forest. The house stands on or near the site of a hunting lodge built by William the Conqueror, which in 1811 was given by George III to his seventh son, the Duke of Cambridge. It was sold by Queen Victoria to her ward, Miss Mabel Walker, the orphan heiress to a Nottinghamshire coal-mining fortune. Following her marriage to Captain Lionel Munro RN, the family name became Munro-Walter. In 1888 they demolished the old house and built the present hundred room house using many of the old materials. It was used for Army training during the War, then became a school. By 1981 it was empty and in danger of falling into decay. It is now a hotel owned by the Virgin Group and has been completely refurbished.

The Ornamental Drive, Rhinefield, where Victorian taste found full expression in the planting of groves of ornamental trees, including many exotic species. Although now popular with visitors, I have heard it disapproved of by those who think it foreign to the native Forest habitat.

Above St Nicholas church, Brockenhurst. Brockenhurst was surrounded by military camps for colonial troops throughout the First World War, and over a hundred of them – New Zealanders, Indians and a Canadian – are buried and commemmorated in the graveyard. Nearby, below his own picturesque headstone, lies Brusher Mills, the famous snake-catcher.

Above right St John's, Boldre, a fine medieval church on a hill. The church is most associated with William Gilpin, its rector from 1777- 1804, who is buried in the church. The quotation on the back cover of this book is from Gilpin, who did more than anyone to make people aware of the beauty of the New Forest. The church contains a memorial to the 1,416 lives that were lost following the sinking of HMS Hood in 1941, and a Memorial Service is still held annually in May.

Right All Saints, Minstead, with the grave of Sir Arthur Conan Doyle (1869-1930), creator of Sherlock Holmes, in the foreground. Conan Doyle bought a house in the village late in his life as a holiday home. The interior of the church is a delightful mixture of a theatre and church, with a triple-decker pulpit and two tiers of galleries.

A typical small-holder's thatched cottage at Bartley, a scattered hamlet right on the edge of the Forest.

Cottages at Gritnam, one of the areas mentioned in the Domesday Book, but now a small isolated hamlet near Bank.

Thatchers at work on a cottage at Swan Green.

Sway Tower, a 128 feet high Forest landmark from the age of eccentricity. The tower was built between 1879 and 1885 as an early experiment with concrete by A.T.T. Peterson, a retired judge, who wanted to prove what conrete was capable of. No scaffolding was used; the concrete was cast in small sections and lifted into place by a crane inside the tower. A climb of 330 steps brings you to the top, where Peterson wanted to put a light but was prevented from doing so because it might have been a danger to shipping.

THE WESTERN BORDERS

THE WESTERN BORDERS

The Conqueror declared the western boundary of the Forest to be the river Avon – the grandest river of the south of England. It gathers its waters across the wide chalk massif of Salisbury Plain, breaks successively from a thousand springs, then pulls its skirts together opposite Salisbury Cathedral and slides down to the sea.

The word Avon simply means river, so it has always been known by a succession of names according to where on its banks people lived – the Wiltshire Avon, the Salisbury Avon, the Hampshire Avon, the Christchurch Avon.

Over sixty years ago I was one of those who came from all over the country to fish the finest mixed-angling water of all. The salmon and sea-trout ran up from the mouth. The roach and chub were enormous. There were shoals of dace each close to the record weight, and grayling twice as big as I had ever seen. One day, near to Fordingbridge, a Birmingham angler caught the biggest pike ever to come from a British river – using a two-pound roach for bait.

Previous page The medieval bridge over the River Avon at Fordingbridge. From the 'Fighting Cocks' at Godshill on the edge of the Forest a steep hill slopes down to the 'Greyhound', beloved of anglers, over the bridge that changed the name of the town. William the Conqueror's clerks who compiled the Domesday Book knew the place just as Forde. Here the famous Avon fishing punts used to lie, and Mrs Frampton used to keep a pot warm night and day so fishermen could feed themselves whenever they came in from the river.

The Saxon church of St Mary, Breamore. Despite alterations, it still has the shape and character of a Saxon village church, and the recent removal of plaster has shown that the walls were once painted with woodland landscapes.

Breamore House. Twenty Saxon manors in the Avon valley had all their east bank lands afforested by the Conqueror when he created the New Forest. In later years, as the power of the throne waned, most of them got it back again. One was the Hulse estate at Breamore, where a glorious brick and stone mansion was built during the reign of the first Queen Elizabeth. Visitors also now know it for the wonderful Carriage and Countryside Museums.

In 1066 there were more than twenty Saxon manors down the main Avon channel. William took away all their land on the eastern bank, thousands of acres of pasture and woodland. However the power of the monarchy has not been constant and from time to time – in the troubled Plantagenet era, for instance – that land was taken back again. This is why there are today many Avon Valley holdings that can still claim common rights in the Forest. But the Avon Valley is still a charming place, although the demands on it are considerable. The wonderful water-meadows along its flood plain were ploughed up in the War to grow corn and its water supply has suffered from the pillaging of the springs.

At Breamore is a fine Elizabethan manor – famous now for its two great collections, the Countryside Museum and the Carriage Museum – which must have won back land across the water.

At Burgate Manor the water still runs through a Jacobean eel-house where the housemaid stood on a stone with a net and fished out the dinner.

At Fordingbridge – once called Forde until someone built a bridge and produced its contradictory name – it can be seen how the whole town developed westward after the land opposite had been taken away.

At Ringwood, every Wednesday for centuries, the commoners drove their carts down to the Cattle Market, to buy and sell stock and supplies and to meet friends from all over the Forest. Sadly that has now disappeared under development; but, despite its girdle of by-passes and fly-overs, old Ringwood still has great character. The stall-holders still come to the triangle of cobbles on market-day and the side-streams of the Avon provide water gardens in the town.

The Avon Valley from above Bicton Mill, one of the great loops made by the Avon on its journey from Salisbury to the sea. In medieval times the river drew a wriggling line between two Royal hunting grounds: the New Forest of William I, and Cranborne Chase to its west, where King John built a hunting lodge.

Breamore Mill astride the Avon. When I fished here long ago they used to tell me of the 8th Baronet who sat here fishing for salmon accompanied by his old retriever. Whenever he hooked a fish the dog took to the river and retrieved it for him, sparing the need for a landing net.

CAPRIOLO
LICENSED
RESTAURANT
TOOLS TOOLS TOOLS
BANANAS
FROM THE
WINDWARD ISLES

Left The Wednesday market in Ringwood, on the western edge of the Forest. For centuries the commoners drove their ponies down to this triangle of cobbles at the end of the High Street for Market Day. A separate cattle market was eventually built, to be recently overwhelmed by development. But the Wednesday market still preserves its sense of occasion, and the old town centre has kept its character.

Above Commoners stock at Woodgreen, the only place where the original boundaries of the New Forest still touch the River Avon.

A mural of cidermaking in the Village Hall at Woodgreen and (left) a general view of the interior of the Hall. In 1931 two students at the Royal College of Art were commissioned to decorate the newly-built village hall. They chose to depict life in the village throughout the seasons, using portraits of more than seventy of the villagers. Other scenes include Morris dancing, the flower show, poaching and fruit-picking.

TIMBER

I think I can say that, apart from the silviculturalists, nobody was ever pleased to see conifers planted on the Forest – except perhaps the sparrowhawk. Unlike other diving hawks he overtakes his prey at flashing speed in level flight; the open rides and spaced bare trunks of the pine-woods are his perfect hunting-ground. Particularly at times when the pigeons are fledging and you can see patches of white feathers here and there on the woodland floor – each one below the spot where a sparrowhawk pranged a young ring-dove.

But that is just a small sub-plot in the long drama of disagreement that has been played out between foresters and forest-dwellers.

Within three centuries of the original afforestment the Kings' need for large herds of venison on the hoof had faded. Agriculture had greatly advanced even by then – and beef was continuously available. Deer became a sporting animal. The nationwide staff of the Lord Warden of the Forests could not be maintained just for sporting purposes.

But if the Kings no longer needed deer, they always needed money. Already the Kings' Salterns at Lymington were exporting salt, even to foreign countries. Next it was the turn of the Forest to show a profit. Thus the foresters became timber-men.

The first Order was for the creation of 'copses' – enclosures of small trees cut down to stools that grew as a forest of poles. The poles were used for charcoal needed for the furnaces and the making of gunpowder. The brushwood tops were tied into 'faggots' that went away in boatloads to the bread ovens of the cities.

Of course, the copses had to be fenced against both deer and cattle. The commoners became alarmed about the reduction of their grazing.

Next the hardwoods, which had previously been taken from 'pollards' – single oaks and beeches cut to form a spreading head that did not need fencing – began to be enclosed. Over three centuries the hardwood trade grew for housebuilding and for the shipyards.

Each order for further enclosure caused local anxiety. Sometimes the orders were so remote from local reality that the foresters themselves combined with commoners to evade them. At one time the proposals for 'rolling enclosure' – as each wood matured and the fences were taken down another planting could be put in hand – seemed to suggest that in the end the whole area would be taken.

The nineteenth century brought the conifers, and the fellings of two World Wars seemed to justify further planting.

By now the old Office of Woods had disappeared, and the management of the New Forest management passed to the Forestry Commission which, charged with operating at a profit, had a great appetite for turning timber into a cash-crop.

Previous page The voice of the Forest changed when the sound of the axe was replaced by that of the chainsaw. But the Forest still produces a skilled team of axemen who travel the shows competing with forest gangs from parts of the British Isles. This photograph shows the forester's tools: his chainsaw, axe, hard hat and gloves.

An old 'pollard', the Knightwood Oak, one of the oldest trees in the New Forest. It was cut early in life so that its branches emerged at the same level. Originally, the head would have spread wider, but some of the pollarded branches were cut as they were needed.

The crisis came when thirty years ago the Commission under cover of theories about regeneration, sent the chainsaws into the ancient woodlands. The outrage was not diminished by an unwary statement from one official that at last they had the liberty to exploit the old woodlands.

Thus the anxiety and hostility of this timber debate rumbled on from the time of the first copses until 1971, when the then Minister of Agriculture ordered an end to hardwood felling. In a following Mandate a ten-year plan for management was introduced and has subsequently been renewed.

Since then the voice of conservation has perhaps become the most powerful local influence.

Thinning oaks in Milkham Inclosure. Once, gangs of foresters would have stripped the thinned trunks of their bark, which was then used for dressing leather in the tanneries.

A forester cutting a square field gate-post out of a round length of oak.

Above Modern charcoal burning in King's Garn Gutter Inclosure. It was started in 1991 as an experiment by the New Forest Charcoal Company after a permit was granted by the Forestry Commission.

Above right Old alder coppice at Holmhill. Alder was widely used for making charcoal. The poles were cut and stacked into a pyramid and then heaped with earth to exclude air. The long slow burning process produced fine quality charcoal for iron smelting and making gunpowder. During the Second World War alder was coppiced to provide charcoal filters for gas masks.

Right A sparrowhawk, the bird of the pine woods. The bare trunks and open rides of the conifer plantations provide the sparrowhawk with an ideal hunting ground.

A demonstration of fire-fighting during a Forestry Commission Open Day. An area the size of the New Forest, which is enjoyed by millions of visitors a year, is always in danger from fire.

Foresters using a crane to look for storm damage in Holidays Hill Inclosure so as to assess which trees still need felling.

Top The industrial workhorse of the Forest, the Scandanavian £100,000 scarifier that prepares the ground for planting in the inclosures.

Above Stripping conifer of its bark. Millions of fencing posts and tree stakes are sold from the conifer inclosures, and the bark is bagged and sold in garden centres as a mulch.

Left Forestry Commission keepers checking a sparrowhawk's nest, a bird whose numbers increase as the conifer plantations reach maturity.

Planting oak seedlings in Set Thorns Inclosure. The tree shelters encourage growth and provide protection against deer and rabbits.

A forester felling a Sitka spruce, a tree which does well in the wetter Forest inclosures. Since the early nineteenth century the Scots, Weymouth and Corsican pine, as well as the Norway spruce, larch and Douglas fir have all been introduced into the Forest. The conifers have enriched the bird life, encouraging Crossbills, Redpolls, Siskins, Goldcrests, Treecreepers and the Hawfinch – which loves the tall tops of the Douglas fir. At the same time, as the canopy has closed over, excluding light, life on the forest floor has withered away. Although the conifer plantations in the New Forest are much more diverse than most, there is a strong ground-swell of opinion in favour of returning the commercial conifer plantations to broad-leafed trees.

PEOPLE IN THE FOREST

PEOPLE IN THE FOREST

In the Introduction I used a phrase often applied to the New Forest – 'The largest area of untouched wilderness in the south of England'. Throughout the rest of the book I think I have shown this to be untrue.

Wilderness is land that has been unaffected by the presence of man. Almost every square yard of the Forest was made what it is today by man's activities. The place is not a wilderness: it is a history book.

It is the history of people, for seven centuries just a few people – a handful of palaeolithic huntsmen, a small tribe of Bronze Age cultivators, then the foresters, the commoners, the gentry who served the King, the monks of Beaulieu and the boatmen of Lymington. At any one time they must all have known one another.

When better roads were built and the skills of carriage-making perfected, the numbers of those living in the Forest increased. The railway in its turn brought the late Victorians to establish themselves in some impressive houses. The waggonettes took the first holidaymakers out among the trees. The old Lord Montagu of Beaulieu bought a new-fangled 'horseless carriage' and invited the Prince of Wales down to take a ride in it.

Previous page A group of children walking in the woods. One great benefit of the New Forest is that it is a wonderful place for learning. For thousands of children, many from the cities, it is their first taste of the great outdoors.

The New Forest Museum, Lyndhurst. In the foreground is a model of Alice Liddell, the original for Lewis Carroll's *Alice in Wonderland*. Alice grew up to become Mrs Reginald Hargreaves and her ashes are buried in the Hargreaves family vault in Lyndhurst churchyard.

The National Motor Museum, Beaulieu. The late Lord Montagu was a motoring pioneer, and the present Viscount established the National Motor Museum in memory of his father. It contains over 200 cars and lorries, providing a fascinating insight into the history of transport.

The future of the New Forest is also concerned with people – but people measured in millions. Already eighteen million live within an hour and a half's journey. Already, on a summer's day, you can assume that twenty-five thousand cars have turned off the roads into the Forest. Although there are now big caravan-sites, the Forestry Commission frequently have to issue a warning in advance of a weekend that all places are already booked.

The trackways are breaking down under the shoes of hired horses. The little fields of small commoners' holdings – which they must occupy in order to hold forest rights – have been sold for vast sums to keep ponies in. Without the commoners' animals the character of the New Forest would soon fade away. Its character is precious and now unique. The other royal forests – with which it once formed a system – have been broken up and distributed, most of them more than a hundred years ago. The Mandate that followed the critical visit of the Minister of Agriculture in 1971 stated that the guarding of this character must be the first purpose of future management.

I look back, past all I have seen happen since, to a summer night in 1928 when, for the first time, I was travelling west on a cycling holiday. I ran my bike into the backside of a pony that was dozing on the old Ringwood road. Landing unharmed in a soft bush of heather I sat in the quiet darkness and listened to its hoofs cantering off down a track.

May the future history of the New Forest be governed with wisdom and consideration – no matter how many people it now has to serve.

Until recently the donkey was the transport of the poorer Forest residents. One old man told me that his donkey, which took him weekly to 'The Old English Gentleman' at Lymington, was 'the fastest trottin' moke' in the Forest. A few of their descendants still remain, and can be seen here enjoying a visitors picnic.

The Portugese Fireplace, west of Lyndhurst. The New Forest played an important role in the First World War. Manoeuvres were held on the heath, camps and airfields were set up, even the heather was gathered for packing ammunition. Its timber was invaluable, and the forestry workers were helped by a Portugese Army Unit, who manned a lumber camp using steam saws near Emery Down. After the war, their flint cookhouse fireplace was preserved as a memorial to their work. I recall, aged five, watching them drive great six-horse timber waggons and listening to their strange shouts.

Nine hundred years of hunting. From the very beginning the Forest was a hunting ground. The Buckhounds – the only ones in Britain, the Foxhounds and the Beagles are all famous packs. Here the hounds break from a covert to fan out across one of the lawns.

Left A cricket match on Swan Green, which can be thought of as the Village Green of the Forest.

Right Ponies and riders gathered for a Point-to-Point meeting. There are two meetings a year, on Boxing Day and over Easter, but unlike other point-to-points there is no obvious course. Neither the start or finish are announced until the riders gather, and it is as much a test of Forest knowledge as skill on horseback.

Below The skills of carriage driving were revived in the Forest by Sanders Watney of Bisterne Close, brewer and coachmaster. The British Driving Society now thrives all over Britain. Elegant carriages from the past that used to lie rotting are now precious again. This is a meeting of the Pony and Trap Club near Lucy Hill.

Top Caravaners at Ashurst caravan site, one of a ten such sites in the Forest. Last year some 750,000 camper nights were spent in the Forest, providing a valuable source of revenue for its management.

Above The Lymington River on a summer's day in August.

Right The gardens at Exbury House. The gardens were started by Lionel de Rothchild, who bought the house in 1919 and began establishing a large woodland garden on the acid soil. It now covers 250 acres, with rare trees forming a background to the huge collections of rhododendrons, azaleas and other acid loving plants that make it such a mass of colour.

THE PHOTOGRAPHS

All the photographs for this book were taken using Nikon equipment. The majority of the landscapes using a Nikkor zoom 24-50mm f3.3 lens, and the smaller forms of wildlife and plants with a Macro Nikkor 105mm f2.8. For birds and mammals I prefer either a Nikkor ED 300mm f4.5 lens or a Nikkor ED 500mm f5.5. A tripod may be cumbersome but it is essential. I try to restrict the use of filters, but in some cases they are necessary, and I use a polarising filter together with a graduated blue and grey.

Photographing the sheer diversity of landscapes and wildlife in the New Forest makes local knowledge of the Forest very important, but nothing is as vital is merely keeping your eye open. You may spot a deer, but if your camera is still in its bag it is more than likely that by the time you are ready to photograph it the deer will have vanished.

In general terms, the wildlife is best photographed in the early morning, when the light is softer and many of the mammals are feeding. Despite the number of visitors to the Forest, there are still quiet places where you will be undisturbed. The mammals require patience. The photograph of the foxes was the result of spending forty hours with the same family over a season.

I think the woods are best photographed in the autumn. The light is good, the leaves give colour, and there is a general atmosphere of mellow fruitfulness.

I have taken literally tens of thousands of photographs of the New Forest over the years. Many more have had to be specially taken for this book. The business of selecting and reducing the numbers to the final choice is never easy, but I hope that those we have included give you as much pleasure to look at as they have given me to take.

TERRY HEATHCOTE

ACKNOWLEDGEMENTS

Very many people have helped to create this book, and our thanks are due to all of them. Our first debt is to the people of the New Forest, and visitors to it, who are depicted in the book, either wittingly or unwittingly. The seed for the book was sown by Gordon Young of Kings of Lymington, and we are grateful to him for his support.

We would also like to thank Mrs Shirley Blick, Clerk to the Verderer's Court, and the New Forest Agisters for their assistance. In addition, and more generally, we are indebted to the Forestry Commission - especially the keepering staff - for their willingness over the years to share their deep knowledge of the Forest.

We are also grateful to the following for allowing us to take photographs: The New Forest Museum and Visitors Centre, The National Motor Museum, Woodgreen Village Hall, Ted Penny, Peter Brown and Miss Louise Dobbs for the map.

The following books have been invaluable to Jack Hargreaves when researching the text: the magisterial *The New Forest* by Colin Tubbs, and Terry Heathcote's own book on the Forest, *A Wild Heritage*.

Terry Heathcote's final debt is to his wife Vivienne for her help and patience - particularly when the alarm jingles yet again at five a.m.

TERRY HEATHCOTE AND JACK HARGREAVES

INDEX

Aldridgehill, Ober Water.